GRAPHIC MYTHICAL HEROES

ODYSSEUS AND THE ODYSSEY

BY GARY JEFFREY
ILLUSTRATED BY ALESSANDRO POLUZZI

Gareth Stevens
Publishing

Please visit our website, www.garethstevens.com.
For a free color catalog of all our high-quality books, call toll free 1-800-542-2595 or fax 1-877-542-2596.

Library of Congress Cataloging-in-Publication Data

Jeffrey, Gary.
Odysseus and the Odyssey / Gary Jeffrey.
p. cm. — (Graphic mythical heroes)
Includes index.
ISBN 978-1-4339-7520-2 (pbk.)
ISBN 978-1-4339-7521-9 (6-pack)
ISBN 978-1-4339-7519-6 (library binding)
1. Homer. Odyssey—Juvenile literature. 2. Odysseus (Greek mythology)—Juvenile literature. I. Title.
BL820.O3J44 2012
398.20938'02—dc23

2011045578

First Edition

Published in 2013 by
Gareth Stevens Publishing
111 East 14th Street, Suite 349
New York, NY 10003

Designed by David West Books

Photo credits:
p4r, shakko

Printed in China

CPSIA compliance information: Batch #DWS12GS: For further information contact Gareth Stevens, New York, New York at 1-800-542-2595.

CONTENTS

A Fateful Wanderer

Odysseus was the legendary king of Ithaca and one of the Greek leaders during the Trojan War. After spending ten years fighting alongside other heroes, like Achilles, he set sail for home with 12 ships, each carrying 50 men. The *Odyssey*, by the ancient Greek poet Homer, is the story of that journey.

Quick witted and silver-tongued, Odysseus was the brains behind the wooden horse that allowed the Greeks to sneak into Troy and capture the city.

A Hopeless Start

While trying to raid the Cicones in Thrace, the Ithacans were attacked and driven out to sea. Blown by storms, they reached an island off North Africa.

The people on the island did nothing but eat a plant called the lotus flower and sleep. When an Ithacan landing party tasted the flower, they became drugged and lost all interest in getting home. Odysseus was forced to kidnap them and ordered all his men to set sail right away to save them from the fate of the lotus-eaters.

In a matter of a few months, Odysseus expected to be reunited with his queen, Penelope (right), and son Telemachus, but it was not to be.

Odysseus and his men sneaked past the blinded cyclops by hiding among his flock of sheep.

Land of the Cyclopes

Next they landed on the island of the sons of Poseidon—the legendary cyclopes. Odysseus's curiosity to see how these one-eyed giants lived caused him and 11 others to be trapped in the cave of a cyclops called Polyphemus. The cannibal giant ate four of his men before Odysseus devised a cunning plan to get away by blinding him.

After the cyclops episode, Odysseus was gifted all the winds except the west wind by Aeolus, the ruler of winds. Odysseus slept as the fleet approached Ithaca, and his crew mistakenly opened the bag of winds, blowing them back to where they had started.

On Lamos, a race of giant cannibals attacked the Ithacans. All the ships except Odysseus's were destroyed.

Circe's Isle

After the attack on Lamos, Odysseus and his last remaining ship sailed to the island of Aeaea, home of the famed sorceress Circe. Odysseus sent twenty men to find Circe. At her house, she offered them wine, secretly mixed with a potion designed to stun them…

THE ODYSSEY

FROM CIRCE TO SCYLLA AND CHARYBDIS

...INTO PIGS!

NOW OFF TO THE STY WITH YOU!

SQUEEEEEEEEE!

ONLY EURYLOCHUS, WHO HAD WAITED OUTSIDE, WAS SPARED...

ODYSSEUS, THE CREW - **CIRCE'S BEWITCHED THEM ALL!**

AS AN ARMED ODYSSEUS STRODE TOWARD CIRCE'S HOUSE, THE GOD HERMES APPEARED BEFORE HIM.

ODYSSEUS, EAT SOME OF THIS SPECIAL HERB. IT WILL **PROTECT** YOU FROM CIRCE'S MAGIC.

AS ODYSSEUS DRANK THE WINE THAT CIRCE HAD GIVEN HIM, SHE TOUCHED HIM WITH HER STICK.
SLURRRP!
NOW OFF TO THE STY...
...WITH YOU?
HA! HA! HA! HA!
SCHLINK!

Y-YOU MUST BE **ODYSSEUS!**
YOUR ARRIVAL WAS **FORETOLD**.
RELEASE MY CREW, OR I WILL RELEASE YOU FROM YOUR **LIFE**.
FORGIVE MY RUDENESS. I WILL UNDO THE SPELL.

NOW WE'VE BEEN INTRODUCED, LET ME ENTERTAIN ALL OF YOU.

OINK?

ODYSSEUS TOLD CIRCE OF THEIR JOURNEY SO FAR.

...AND SO ANY HELP YOU CAN OFFER...

I KNOW THE WAY TO THE LAND OF **THE DEAD.**

YOU MUST GO THERE AND TALK TO A BLIND PROPHET CALLED **TIRESIAS....**

"...HE HAS IMPORTANT INFORMATION ABOUT YOUR JOURNEY."
ODYSSEUS, THERE IS NO PLACE SO BLEAK AS **THE UNDERWORLD...**
BRING THE RAMS...
THE RAMS' BLOOD WAS POURED INTO THE TRENCH. THE BLOOD WOULD ENABLE THE DEAD TO SPEAK. THE PROPHET TIRESIAS WAS A **SHADE**.

THE SCENT OF THE BLOOD CALLED UP MANY SHADES.
LOOK, THERE'S ACHILLES!
AND AJAX!
ODYSSEUS HELD THEM ALL BACK WITH HIS SWORD, UNTIL TIRESIAS HAD DRUNK SOME OF THE BLOOD.
YOU WILL COMPLETE YOUR JOURNEY, ODYSSEUS, BUT IT WILL BE HARD.
ESPECIALLY ON YOUR CREW...

WHEN YOU BLINDED THE CYCLOPS, YOU ANGERED POSEIDON - POLYPHEMUS WAS HIS FAVORITE SON.
THE EARTH SHAKER WILL PLAN TO PUNISH YOU.
WHEN YOU REACH THE LAND OF THRINACIA, DO NOT TOUCH THE GIANT CATTLE THERE, NO MATTER HOW HUNGRY YOU ARE. THEY ARE GUARDED BY ZEUS.
YOU KILL THEM AT YOUR PERIL.

ODYSSEUS RETURNED TO AEAEA TO BID FAREWELL TO CIRCE.

THERE ARE DIFFICULT CHALLENGES BEFORE YOU REACH HELIOS.

BUT I WILL TELL YOU HOW TO OVERCOME THEM.

YOU REALLY ARE THE MOST ***HELPFUL*** WITCH I'VE EVER ENCOUNTERED.

AS DAWN'S ROSY FINGERS CARESSED THE SKY, ODYSSEUS WALKED THE LENGTH OF THE SHIP, GIVING EACH MAN BEESWAX TO PRESS IN HIS EARS.

THEN HE PREPARED HIMSELF TO BE TIED TO THE MAST...

...THE ONLY MAN TO HEAR THE SIRENS' SONG AND *LIVE* TO TELL ABOUT IT.

THE SIRENS WERE BIRDWOMEN WHOSE EERIE CALL LURED UNWARY SAILORS UNFAILINGLY TOWARD THE ROCKS.

ODYSSEUS, CAPTIVATED BY THE SOUND, STRAINED AT HIS BONDS.

CUT ME FREE. I MUST STEER THE SHIP TOWARD THEM!

AAAAH...SUCH SWEET MUSIC...

BUT THE CREW ROWED STEADILY ON, LEAVING THE SIRENS EMPTY-HANDED.

THE SIRENS WERE PASSED, BUT DANGER STILL LURKED AHEAD...

HELMSMAN, YOU SEE AHEAD WHERE THE WATER IS ***RIPPLING?***

AYE

STEER AWAY FROM IT.
KEEP TIGHT TO THE LAND
ON THE LEFT AT ALL COSTS.
THE RIPPLING WAS WHERE CHARYBDIS, A DEADLY WHIRLPOOL, ROSE AND FELL - A DEATH TRAP FOR ANY SHIP THAT GOT CAUGHT IN IT.
MEN, WHEN I GIVE THE SIGNAL, ROW! ROW HARD, HARDER THAN EVER BEFORE!

AS THEY APPROACHED THE CAVE, A LOW MOANING SOUND CAME OUT OF IT.
ROOAAAARMMMM!

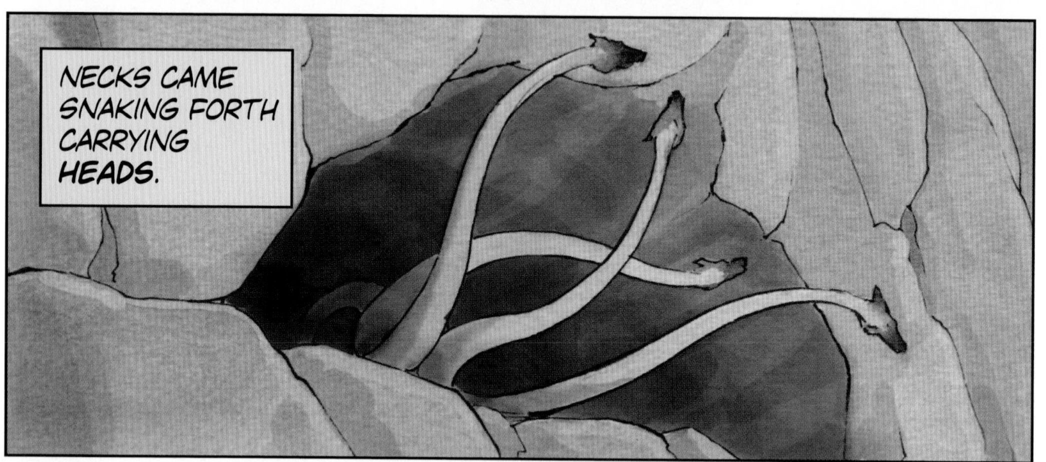
NECKS CAME SNAKING FORTH CARRYING **HEADS.**

SIX HEADS FULL OF **TEETH...**
GRAAAGH!
SNARL!

CLANG!
AAAAAGH!
NOW, ROW! ROW AS IF YOUR LIVES DEPEND ON IT!
CRUNCH!
CIRCE HAD TOLD ODYSSEUS HOW THE MONSTER, SCYLLA, COULD NOT BE KILLED, ONLY OUTRUN. HAD THEY STOOD AND FOUGHT, THEY WOULD HAVE BEEN DOOMED LIKE ALL THOSE BEFORE.
ODYSSEUS AND MOST OF HIS CREW MADE IT THROUGH TO CONTINUE THEIR EPIC JOURNEY HOME.

Becalmed at Thrinacia, Odysseus's men ignored his orders and slew the giant cattle of the sun god, Helios. Outraged, Helios cried for revenge, and Zeus sent a thunderbolt down to the ship, blowing it to pieces, killing all except Odysseus.

A Love Slave

Odysseus was washed up on the island of Ogygia, the home of the nymph Calypso. She was the daughter of Atlas, the Titan who holds up the sky. Calypso fell in love with Odysseus and kept him prisoner for seven years, until he built a raft to leave.

Now Poseidon exacted his revenge by smashing the raft in a storm, washing the bedraggled hero onto the mythical land of Phaeacia. Odysseus told the Phaeacians his story and was finally delivered to Ithaca.

Fate of the Suitors

Before he went to the palace, Odysseus disguised himself as an old beggar. In the 20 years he had been away, things had gotten very difficult for Queen Penelope. More than 100 young suitors set up home at the palace, competing with each other to be the new king, if only Penelope would choose them.

Odysseus's final act was to join forces with Telemachus, his son. They slayed the suitors and reclaimed his kingdom. The story ends with him reunited with his wife, his odyssey ended.

Odysseus kills the suitors with his bow and arrow.

GLOSSARY

bedraggled Messy after having gotten wet.

bleak Grim, dark, or depressing.

cannibal A human or animal that eats other members of its own species.

caressed Stroked gently in a caring manner.

cyclops A giant monster with one eye.

foretold Predicted, revealed ahead of time.

lured Tricked or tempted into going to a certain place.

odyssey A long journey filled with danger and adventure.

peril The risk of danger.

raid To attack a city and steal its people's valuables.

shade The spirit of someone who has died.

sty A muddy pen in which pigs are kept.

unwary Not aware or not paying attention.

Index